LEARN FRENCH

French Words
With Foreign Origins

French Word Origins
To Grow
Your French Vocabulary
For English Speakers

By   NEO URBAN TONGUE

Learn FRENCH - French Words With Foreign Origins
French Word Origins To Grow Your French Vocabulary For English Speakers

This document is brought to you by NEO URBAN TONGUE

Cover image "Tongue " - courtesy of iStockphoto.com

Paperback ISBN: **9798377865230**
Hardback ISBN: **9798853232570**
© **Neo Urban Tongue, 2023**
Paris, France
Imprimé à la demande
Dépôt légal : Février 2023 n° *10000000858487*
ISBN livre broché : **9798377865230**
ISBN livre relié :   **9798853232570**

CONTENT

Who Should Read this Book

Are you an English speaker wanting to learn French, particularly to understand French words/phrases with foreign origins?

Are you tired of the traditional approach to language learning?

Are you curious about enjoying a more original approach to discovering a language?

Do you often feel like an outsider in French-speaking conversational contexts?

Are you looking to break down those language barriers and connect more with the French speakers you meet on holiday, at work, or even online?

If you answered YES to any of the above questions, this book is for **YOU**.

Do you prefer traditional language learning methods via grammar and learning by heart?

Are you more attracted to a purist and classical approach to learning the French language?

Even if this is the case, **we think you'll still find value in this book**.

My Promise to You

I hear you.

You've had it with classical French Language-Learning material. Same old format, the usual overkill when it comes to grammar content.

You start off full of enthusiasm, and it's only a matter of time before you're saturated and hit a wall, and abandon your learning process.

This e-Book is here to <u>complement</u> your Language Learning Journey.

It will provide you with a deeper knowledge of French by reading around the subject. Its format will make it easier to remember and to join the dots between French and other languages.

Let's go!

Introduction

French is a beautiful language, and it is a language that matters: it is spoken by 275 million [1] people on this planet.

If you currently live in a French-speaking environment, then mastering the language is also one step toward better integration. However, most people who learn French are not necessarily living in a French-speaking environment.

Whether you are starting your French language learning journey or have already acquired a certain level of knowledge in the French language, going off the beaten track can be a source of motivation and inspiration.

Learning about the origins of a language can even give you an insight into the roots of your *own* language.

The number of words in a particular language can seem astronomical. Whichever figure is quoted can be debatable. In reality, people tend to use a limited number of words on a day-to-day basis. Take English and French:

Language	Nbr of actual words vs. frequently used words	Source
English	470,000 vs 3,000	Oxford English Dictionary, Merriam-Webster
French	300,000 vs 3,000	Le Petit Robert

Fortunately for us, there are many obvious links when comparing French to another language. This is mainly thanks to **cognates**: words with a similar or identical spelling, pronunciation, and meaning.

To illustrate this with a few non-exhaustive examples, let us compare French with English. Often, but not always, words ending in '**tion**', '**al**', '**ance**', '**ber**', '**ble**', '**ence**', '**ic**', '**or**', and '**ty**' can have a similar or identical spelling to the equivalent French word.

e.g.

*la communica**tion**, le festiv**al**, la fin**ance**,*
*le nom**bre**, horri**ble**, la confér**ence**,*
*mus**ique**, le doct**eur**, l'étern**ité**.*

The English equivalents are obvious.

This book is NOT just a list of words - it provides the context in which featured words are used in the French language.

A Melting Pot

French is a vibrant language and is one of the Romance languages, which include Italian, Spanish, Catalan, Portuguese, Romanian, and Romansch, spoken by people in Switzerland, bordering Italy. When you consider the number of neighbouring[2] countries to France, its ancient and colonial history, immigration, and the more globalized world we live in, you can imagine the diversity of influences coming from other languages.

In addition to French, France has other officially recognized languages[3], each having its own influences. These include:

> Breton, Normand, Flamand, Basque, Catalan, Occitan, Corsican, Savoyard, Franc-Comtois & Alsation.

This book will allow you to gain insight into a number of origins of the French Language and hopefully discover that French is very much an accessible language.
It can be surprising how many similarities and links there are between French and other languages.
You never know. As you read this book, there may be a few *'Aha moments*' to savour.

How this Book is Structured

This book will cover French word origins from a variety of languages. These will be grouped into sections in the following way:

- Italian, Spanish, and Portuguese
- German and English
- Arabic
- Greek and Latin
- And some other less obvious origins

You'll discover some of the links between French and these languages. In general, the French word will appear in bold, followed by the word in the language of origin and English. An explanation of the term will follow, as will a number of derived words.

For conciseness, various abbreviations *(abbr.)* will be used:

(Fr.) French	*(It.)* Italian
(Sp.) Spanish	*(Por.)* Portuguese
(Ger.) German	*(Eng.)* English
(Ar.) Arabic	*(Gr.)* Greek
(Lat.) Latin	*(Nor.)* Old Norse
(Jap.) Japanese	*(Hin.)* Hindi
(n.) noun	*(v.)* verb
(adj.) adjective	*(adv.)* adverb
(nm.) masculine noun	*(nf.)* feminine noun
(sing.) singular	*(pl.)* plural

Are you ready to go?

CHAPTER 1

Italian Origins

Italy and its Immense Cultural Heritage

Italy is home to an immense cultural heritage that has hugely impacted the world over the centuries.

The Romans [4] were able to conquer swathes of Europe, North Africa, and the Middle East. Of course, they became so overstretched that the decline and collapse of the Empire became inevitable.

However, the Romans certainly left their mark on many countries with their commerce, language, art, political doctrines, architecture, engineering, and fighting strategies.

There are many similarities between modern-day Italian and several other European languages used today, a prominent link being Latin.

These similarities can be evident in the written form, but the pronunciation can be somewhat different.

The Italian language is a trendy[5] language to learn and the Italian culture, both past and present, is a big attraction to many people. In the realm of music, there is a very long list of Italian musical terms that have been adopted as-is by many languages.

Italian Design [6] is reputed to be innovative, avant-garde, cutting-edge, and competitive. It can be seen in Interior Design, Jewellery Design, Architecture[7], the Automotive Industry (Lamborghini, Ferrari, Vespa), Car Brand design, Fashion, and Ceramics.

The list of French words with Italian origins is very long. Here are just a few:

A capella – a cappella (*It.*) a cappella (*Eng.*)

A Cappella is a term used for singers who are unaccompanied by an instrument.

(*It.*)	(*Fr.*)
la cappella	*la chapelle*

(*Eng.*)	(*Lat.*)
chapel	cappella

e.g.

Les artistes ont fait une interprétation originale de l'œuvre a cappella.
The artists made an original musical performance a cappella.

La banqueroute - la bancarotta *(It.)* bankruptcy *(Eng.)*

La bancarotta [8] *(It.)* is derived from two Italian words:

(It.)	**una banca**
(Fr.)	*une banque*
(Eng.)	bank
(Lat.)	argentaria/ripa

(It.)	**rotta**
(Fr.)	*rompu*
(Eng.)	broken/ruptured
(Lat.)	rumpo

e.g.

Après la crise de 2008, plusieurs banques ont fait banqueroute (ont fait faillite).
After the 2008 crisis, several banks went bankrupt.

La cartouche - la cartuccia *(It.)* cartridge *(Eng.)*

La cartouche can refer to

| *(Fr.)* | une cartouche d'encre |
| *(Eng.)* | ink cartridge |

| *(Fr.)* | une cartouche à balle |
| *(Eng.)* | bullet cartridge/slug round |

(It.)	*(Fr.)*
la carta	*la carte*

(Eng.)	*(Lat.)*
card	carta

e.g.

Les cartouches d'encre de mon imprimante ne durent pas longtemps.
The ink cartridges on my printer don't last very long.

La contrebasse - Il contrabbasso *(It.)*   double-bass *(Eng.)*

(It.)	*(Fr.)*
contra	contre

(Eng.)	*(Lat.)*
against/contrary	contrã

'contrã' implies opposition or inversion.

e.g.

La note jouée par la contrebasse correspond en réalité à une note une octave en dessous de la note indiquée sur la partition.

The actual note played by a double-bass is one octave lower than the note indicated on the score.

Crescendo - crescendo (*It.*) crescendo (*Eng.*)

Crescendo[9] is used to indicate that the music is to be played gradually louder and louder, e.g.

Quelque chose va crescendo (*Fr.*).
crescens (*Lat.*)

Something attains greater heights
or momentum is built up gradually.

La daube – la dobba (*It.*) stew (*Eng.*)

---

coquere, pulmentum (*Lat.*)

(v.) adobar *(It.)* *mariner* (*Fr.*) to marinate (*Eng.*)
marinate (*Lat.*)

(n.) una marinata *(It.)* *une marinade* (*Fr.*)
marinade (*Eng.*)

Laissez mariner la viande dans la sauce.
Leave the meat to marinate in the sauce.

See the recipe for the *Daube Provençale*[10] :
Ragoût de bœuf au vin rouge.
Beef stew marinated in red wine.

Le dessin - Il disegno *(It.)* drawing/sketch *(Eng.)*

dēscriptiõ, graphicē *(Lat.)*

Il disegno *(It.)* corresponds to
le design (Fr.) design *(Eng.)* consilio *(Lat.)*.

The Italian verbs *disegnare + concepire* correspond to

concevoir/créer/dessiner (Fr.) to design *(Eng.)*
confabricor/escogitare *(Lat.)*.

e.g.

Elle a fait un dessin très détaillé.
She made a very detailed drawing.

*Les plans du bâtiment ont été conçus à l'aide de la
CAO (conception assistée par ordinateur).*

The architectural plans have been designed using
CAD (Computer-Aided Design).

La mascarade – la mascherata *(It.)* masquerade *(Eng.)*

La mascherata[11] means a charade or pretence *(Eng.).*

e.g.

Il vaut mieux que cette mascarade cesse le plus tôt possible.
It would be better if this masquerade ended as soon as possible.

(It.)	*(Fr.)*
la maschera	*le masque*

(Eng.)	*(Lat.)*
mask	persõna

e.g.

La Mascherata est un rassemblement festif de gens qui portent un masque pour dissimuler le visage.
The *Mascherata* is a festive gathering of people who wear a mask (*la Maschera*) to hide their faces.

La perruque – la parrucca (*It.*) wig (*Eng*)

---

capillāmentum (*Lat.*)

Le juge porte une perruque.
The judge is wearing a wig.

Piano *(adj.)* piano (*It.*) piano (*Eng*)

A musical term indicating 'to play softly'
diminuer l'intensité sonore (Fr.).

(n.) il pianoforte (*It.*) *le piano* (*Fr.*) the piano *(Eng.)*

(*Fr.*)	*(adj.) (m.) mou, (f.) molle*
(*Eng.*)	soft
(*Lat.*)	mollis

(*Fr.*)	*(adv.) doucement*
(*Eng.*)	softly
(*Lat.*)	molliter, lēniter

Le restaurant – il ristorante *(It.)* restaurant *(Eng.)*

popina, caupona *(Lat.)*

canteen, inn, tavern *(Eng.)*

(Fr.)	*(n.)* la restauration
(Eng.)	catering

(Fr.)	*(n.)* la restauration rapide
(Eng.)	Fast-food

L'industrie de la restauration rapide a été soumise à une pénurie de personnel depuis la fin de la crise.

The Fast Food industry has been subjected to a shortage of staff since the end of the crisis.

Le tempo - il tempo *(It.)* the tempo *(Eng.)*

(Fr.)	*le pas, la démarche*
(Eng.)	the pace
(Lat.)	passus, gradus

(Fr.)	*la paix*
(Eng.)	peace
(Lat.)	pax, pacem

Le tempo : un terme musical utilisé en français et en anglais pour indiquer la vitesse d'exécution d'une œuvre musicale.

17

Tempo: a musical term used in both French and English to indicate the pace at which a musical piece is to be played.

Refer to **MC Solaar**'s hit song from 1991:
Qui sème le vent récolte le tempo [12]

> *Qui sème le vent récolte le tempo.*
> He who sows the wind shall reap the tempo.
> **MC Solaar**

This is a play on words based on a verse from the Old Testament *Hosea (8:7)* [13]

> *Qui sème le vent, récole la tempête.*
> He who sows the wind shall reap the whirlwind.
> **Hosea (8:7)**

CHAPTER 2

Spanish Origins

Spain and its Official Languages

Spain has a rich cultural heritage and a strong national identity. Castillian is the main language, but there are several official languages: Aranese, Basque, Castillian, Catalan, Estremaduran, and Galician.

Links between border regions have always been strong. Several well-known Spanish words have found their way into the French language and have been officially recognized as part of the French language by the illustrious *Académie Française*.

In French regions bordering Spain, there are several languages used today:

Catalan can still be heard in Southern France between the Pyrenees Mountains and Perpignan on the Mediterranean side.

Basque, aka **Euskara**[14], is also a language with a strong identity in France. The Basque region in France is situated along parts of the border with Spain, between Bayonne on the Atlantic coast and communal areas just South-East of the city of Pau. There are strong links with the Basque region in Spain around the Navarre province.

Occitan is a term used to group several regional variants of the same language: Provençale, Languedocian, and Gascon. These are spoken in southern parts of France, spanning from the France-Italian region (Piedmont, Monaco) to the Gascon region, covering South-East France around the Pyrenean region and the Massif Central. They are also considered as *Langues d'Oc* or languages of Occitania.

It's interesting to note the linguistic links between Occitan and Aranese[15], spoken around the Val d'Aran in the Pyrenees on the Spanish side of the mountains.

It was once upon a time integrated into the Kingdom of Aragon, from whence came Catherine of Aragon[16], who was first married to Arthur Tudor and then to his brother, Henry VIII, in 1509.

Here are a few examples of French words with Spanish origins:

> **L'aficionado** - el aficionado *(nm.)* l'aficionada *(nf.) (Sp.)*
> aficionado *(Eng.)*

A fan, a lover of, or someone who is enthusiastic, well-documented and well-informed on a particular subject or theme. *e.g.*

Ceux qui participent aux Ferias sont parfois des aficionados de courses de taureaux.
Some of the people who attend Ferias are passionate about the Running of the Bulls.

> **Bravo !** – ¡Bravo! *(Sp.)*   Bravo! *(Eng.)*

euge *(Lat.)*

This enthusiastic interjection can be a shout or cry to cheer on a comrade or to show one's approval in an exuberant way, e.g. following a musical performance or a speech.

Interesting to note that in Spanish, it can also mean 'fierce', 'bad-tempered', 'courageous', or 'stormy'.

The French use *brave* to describe a person as being 'good', 'nice', 'a brick', 'solid as a rock', or 'someone you can count on' or simply a regular guy or even a kind and simple, endearing man.

> *C'est un brave homme ! - C'est un mec bien.*
> *C'est quelqu'un de gentil.*
>
> He's a top bloke - He's a brick.
> And also 'the salt of the earth'.

Le/la camarade - el camarado *(nm.)* la camarada *(nf.)* *(Sp.)* comrade *(Eng.)*

socius *(Lat.)*

> It refers to someone who is close or a companion,
> friend, colleague, or a fellow-soldier.

e.g.

> *Je pars avec mes camarades de classe.*
> I am leaving with my classmates.

Le charlatan - el charlatán *(nm.)* la charlatana *(nf.) (Sp.)* charlatan *(Eng.)*

A charlatan is also used in English to indicate someone who pretends to have certain skills, but does not possess them.

e.g.

> *Il ne faut pas faire confiance à ce type. C'est un charlatan.*
> Don't trust that guy. He's a charlatan.

In Spanish, this has the same meaning as the above, as well as referring to someone who is a chatterbox.

e.g.

Cette fille est une vraie bavarde.
That girl is such a chatterbox.

L'embargo - el embargo *(Sp.)* embargo *(Eng.)*

L'embargo[17] can have several meanings:
La saisie de propriété.
The seizure of property.

L'embargo – *une forme de punition économique visant un gouvernement ou une organisation, en lui interdisant l'accès à certains aéroports ou ports ou en lui empêchant le commerce de certains biens ou de matières premières.*

Embargo - a form of economic punishment against a government or an organisation, that can include prohibiting access to certain airports or ports or banning the trade of a particular product or raw material.

e.g.

L'Union Européenne a décidé de mettre en œuvre un embargo sur les armes.
The EU has decided to enforce an arms embargo.

(v.) lever l'embargo (Fr.)
to lift the embargo *(Eng.)*

La feria – la feria *(Sp.)* fair, carnival, festival *(Eng.)*

feriã *(Lat.)*   festival, holidays *(Eng.)*

In France, there are several *ferias* in the South. One of the most well-known is *La Feria de Bayonne*[18] or *Les Fêtes de Bayonne* :

e.g.

Elle va à la Feria de Nîmes avec ses potes.
She is going to the Feria in Nimes with her mates.

La fiesta – la fiesta *(Sp.)* fiesta *(Eng.)*

A celebration, a party or a festive gathering of people.

e.g.

La Fiesta de San Fermin (Sp.)
La Feria de San Fermin Pamplune (Fr.)

takes place each year in July in Pamplona, Navarre, in North Western Spain.
This is where the famous Running of The Bulls takes place.

Hemingway was a big fan of the festival, which inspired his book ***Fiesta: The Sun Also Rises*** (1926) [19] .

Ce soir ça va être chaud. On va faire la fiesta !
Tonight is gonna be wild. It's party time!

Le gaspacho - el gazpacho *(Sp.)* gazpacho *(Eng.)*

Gazpacho [20] is a cold and refreshing soup made in the Summer season.

Ingrédients :
tomates, poivron rouge, concombre, oignons, aïl,
vinaigre, huile d'olive, piment, sel et poivre, eau.

Ingredients:
tomatoes, red pepper, cucumber, onions, garlic,
vinegar, olive oil, chili, salt and pepper, water.

see https://neo-urban-tongue.com/list-of-herbs-and-spices/ for a list of Herbs and Spices (French<->English).

e.g.

J'adore le gaspacho pour sa fraîcheur, son goût et sa légèreté.

I love gazpacho for its freshness, its taste, and its lightness.

Le gilet – el jileco, el chaleco *(Sp.)* sleeveless jacket *(Eng.)*

(Fr.)	*le gilet de sauvetage*
(Eng.)	life-jacket
(Fr.)	*un gilet sans manche*
(Eng.)	a sleeveless jacket, tanktop
(Fr.)	*un gilet pare-balles*
(Eng.)	bullet-proof vest

Mettez votre gilet de sauvetage avant de monter à bord.
Put on your life-jacket before you board.

La guérilla – la guerilla (*Sp.*) guerilla (*Eng.*)

(nf.) guerra de guerrillas *(Sp.)*
la guerre de guérilla (Fr.)
guerrilla warfare *(Eng.)*

A form of unconventional (sometimes unofficial) warfare that employs rapid and sudden attacks and retreats, giving the adverse army little or no time to react.

e.g.

Les guérillas ont infligé de lourdes pertes à l'armée.
The guerrillas inflicted great losses on the Army.

(Sp.)	(n.) la guerra
(Fr.)	la guerre
(Eng.)	the war

(Sp.)	(n.) el guerrillero (nm.) la guerrillera (nf.)
(Fr.)	le guérilla, la guérilla
(Eng.)	the guerrilla, paramilitary soldier

(Sp.)	(adj.) guerrillero / guerrillera
(Fr.)	guérilla
(Eng.)	guerrilla

Le hamac – la hamaca (*Sp.*) hammock (*Eng.*)

Hammocks [21] are thought to have been invented by the Incas and the Mayas.

La hamaca *(Sp.)* can also be used for a deckchair or rocking chair.

e.g.

> *Je vais faire une sieste dans le hamac.*
> I'm going to take a nap in the hammock.

Macho *(adj.)* macho *(Sp.)* macho *(Eng.)*

In Spanish and French, *macho* can mean either masculine or macho. In French, it can refer to

(Adj.) mâle, masculin (*Fr.*)
male, masculine (*Eng.*)

also

(Adj.) macho (fr.) - macho *(Eng.)* can be used to depict an assertive man who considers himself superior to women and other men.

(n.) le macho (*Fr.*) the macho (*Eng.*)

Le maïs – el maiz *(Sp.)*   corn *(Eng.)*

Corn [22] is a crop that originated in modern-day Mexico between 6,000-10,000 BC. Before the discovery of the New World, corn was not present in Europe. It was introduced to Europe by Columbus and has become a popular and strategically important staple since its introduction.

(Fr.)	*l'épi de maïs au naturel*
(Eng.)	corn on the cob

(Fr.)	*la fécule*
(Eng.)	starch

(Fr.)	*la fécule de maïs*
(Eng.)	cornflour

Le patio – el patio *(Sp.)*   patio *(Eng.)*

In Spanish, it can refer to a schoolyard, a courtyard often paved with stones or slabs, or the 'orchestra' seats in a theatre.

(Fr.)	*(Eng.)*
une cour	a yard
la cour de récréation, la cour de récré	schoolyard

29

CHAPTER 3

Portuguese Origins

Portugal was a great sea-faring nation from the 1420s onwards. Explorers such as Vasco Da Gama and Ferdinand Magellan made their mark in History. Magellan[23] led an expedition to become the first to circumnavigate the globe. Although he died on the long journey, the first ship completed the journey in 1522.

The Portuguese influence can be felt in many countries: Brazil, Cap Verde, Guinea-Bissau, São Tomé and Principe, Angola, Mozambique, Goa in India, East Timor, and Macao.

The Portuguese had a reputation for Exploration and Trade and introduced many products to Portugal and Europe, including cinnamon and other Eastern spices. They controlled the Spice Trade from the early 1500s.

This included the Moluccas, aka The Spice Islands [24], in modern-day Indonesia. These islands were then seized by the Dutch in 1620.

A growing Portuguese community is spread around France, and their beautiful and distinct language has contributed many words to the French language over the ages. Here are a few:

Le bambou – bambu *(Por.)* bamboo *(Eng.)*

Portuguese merchants first imported *Bambu* into Europe in the 16th century.

Le bambou a des qualités intéressantes pour le développement durable.
Bamboo possesses interesting qualities for sustainable development.

Le cachalot – cachalote *(Por.)* sperm whale *(Eng.)*

Cachalote (Por.) also means 'Big Head'.

Les cachalots peuvent vivre soixante-dix ans ou plus.
Sperm whales can live 70 years or more.

Le cachou – cachu *(Por.)* cachou *(Eng.)*

aka Black Catechu or Khadira.

Une substance noire extraite de l'arbre acacia. Cachou Lajaunie™ est une marque française de pastilles pour rafraîchir l'haleine.

A black substance extracted from the Indian Acacia Tree. Cachou Lajaunie™ is also a French brand of pastels to freshen the breath.

The Tamils call this Kasu.

Le caramel – caramelo *(Por.)* caramel *(Eng.)*

Les français sont friands de crêpes caramel au beurre salé.

The French are quite partial to pancakes with salted caramel.

La caravelle – caravela *(Por.)* caravel *(Eng.)*

Un bateau rapide et manœuvrable, inventé par les portugais au XVe siècle pour naviguer près des côtes africaines.

A rapid and maneuverable ship, invented by the Portuguese in the XV century used to navigate the African coastlines.

Le cobaye – cabuya *(Por.)* guinea pig *(Eng.)*

Le cobaye a été découvert en Amérique latine.
The guinea pig was discovered in Latin America.

Le Japon – Japâo *(Por.)* Japan *(Eng.)*

There are several theories as to the origins of the name Japan [25] . Here are two of them:

Marco Polo fait référence à un peuple provenant de Zipangu dans ses écrits.
Marco Polo (1254-1324) refers to a people from 'Zipangu' in his writings.

Des explorateurs portugais ont atteint le Japon en 1542 et ont retenu le nom 'Jipan'.
Portuguese explorers reached Japan in 1542 and brought back the name of 'Jipan'.

Lusitanie *(Fr.)*   **Lusitânia** *(Por.)*

During the Roman Empire, current-day Portugal and parts of Spanish Estremadura were part of the province of Lusitania.

Lusitanians come from this region. The French still refer to people from Portugal as *lusitaniens/lusitaniennes*.

Le cheval lusitanien [26]

Le cheval lusitanien est une race de cheval élevé au Portugal.
Le cheval lusitanien is a race of horse that is bred in Portugal.

Le mandarin – mandarim *(Por.)* mandarin *(Eng.)*

Used to denote a person of influence or a tangerine.

(Por.)	*(Fr.)*	*(Eng.)*
(v.) mandar	*ordonner/ commander*	to order / to command

(n.) mantrin in Sanskrit is used for a State Advisor or State Councillor - *un conseiller d'état (fr.)*.

La paillotte – palhota *(Por.)* straw hut *(Eng.)*

Un abri couvert de paille situé en bord de mer.
A straw hut used as a shelter on the seashore.

(Por.)	*(Fr.)*	*(Eng.)*	*(Lat.)*
(n.) palha	*la paille*	straw	strãmentum

(Fr.)	*une meule de foin*
(Eng.)	a haystack

(Fr.)	*un chapeau de paille*
(Eng.)	a straw hat

Le foin (Fr.) hay *(Eng.)*

The French expression *homme de paille* has several meanings:
i) - stooge *(Eng.)* - *un larbin, un laquais (Fr.)* someone willing to take the blame in place of the true perpetrator of a crime.

ii) *un homme de paille (Fr.)* - a figurehead is someone who has the title, but not the power to wield it.

Le zèbre – zebra[27] *(Por.)* zebra *(Eng.)*

The Portuguese were the first Europeans to navigate the coasts of Africa. They stumbled upon a striped animal that resembled a certain Donkey found in their homeland, called the *cebro* or *ezevro*.

L'animal sauvage africain a été nommé le zèbre.
The African wild animal was named the *zebra*.

CHAPTER 4

German Origins

The Birth of a Nation

France has had interactions with its Germanic neighbours for several centuries.

Let us not forget that Napoleon [28] (the first one) ran roughshod over many European Nations in the early 1800s, especially over the different Germanic Nations (Principalities, Dukedoms, Prussia, and Austria).

The Franco-Prussian[29] War began on July 19, 1870, when France declared war on Prussia. Napoleon III had been convinced by his generals that with their modern rifles and the new machine gun (*la mitrailleuse*), a rapid victory was within his reach if France moved quickly.

On August 9, 1870, under the command of Emperor Napoleon III, France suffered a crushing defeat at Sedan in Eastern France.

Other military actions took place, but the Prussians were able to invade Paris. They even seized the opportunity to crown the new Kaiser Wilhelm I in Versailles Palace in January 1871.

It was in May 1871 that the final Treaty of Frankfurt was signed, and the Prussian Victory was complete.

There were several significant consequences of this treaty:

- **Alsace and Lorraine were annexed** and absorbed into the new Germany for the next five decades.

- **Thus ended the Second French Empire**, as did the reign of Napoleon III, *Empereur des Français*, Emperor of the French People, 1852-1870.

- **The Third French Republic** or '*La Troisième République*' **came into existence** following much upheaval and a bloody People's uprising during the Paris Commune in 1871.

The war was now over and had put an end to French hegemony in Europe.

Above all, this opened the way for Otto Von Bismarck to realize his dream of founding the German Reich[30], while surfing on the back of an immense Prussian victory.

Germany was created by the unification of several existing Germanic entities, including Bavaria, Hanover, Nassau, Prussia, and Saxony, to name but a few.

The German culture is rich and deep and is known for its industriousness, religious reformations, literature, its sausages, its hugely rich musical heritage, Art throughout the ages, architecture, its mathematicians, its physicists, and its philosophers (Engels, Goethe, Kant, Luxemburg, Nietzsche, Schiller, Schopenhauer - the list goes on).

Above all, for its contrast between its conservatism and its liberalism.

Languages in the France-Germany Border Regions

Besides French, several languages exist along border regions with Luxembourg, Germany, and Switzerland: **Alsation** is a language spoken in the region of Alsace, on the border with today's Germany. It is part of the Alemannic[31] languages, which include Swiss German and Swabian (spoken around Lake Constance). Alsace was re-integrated into the French Republic at the end of WW1.

Franc-Comtois is spoken in the region of Franche-Comté, which borders both Alsace and Switzerland.

Lorrain is spoken in parts of Lorraine, which borders Belgium, Luxembourg, Germany, and Alsace. Each of these languages has been influenced by Germanic languages over the centuries.

Here are a few examples of French words with German origins:

Une chopine/une chope – der Schoppen *(Ger.)* a glass of beer *(Eng.)*

Une chopine est un verre à bière avec un contenu d'à peu près 50 cl. Le terme vient d'un ancien système de mesure de l'époque médiévale en France.

A Chopin is a beer glass with its approximate half-litre content. The term comes from a system of measure used in medieval France.

Ersatz – ersatz *(Ger.)*   ersatz *(Eng.)*

A substitute for the real thing.

e.g.

(Fr.)   *ersatz de café*

           ersatz coffee,

(Eng.)   *coffee substitute*

---

*Un produit de remplacement, d'une qualité
médiocre.*

A substitute product of mediocre quality.

Le glockenspiel - das Glockenspiel *(Ger.)*
glockenspiel *(Eng.)*

The glockenspiel[32] is a metallic percussion instrument with metal bars set up like a piano keyboard. Vertical metal tubes help resonate the sound when the bars are struck with a stick.

Le glockenspiel est un instrument de percussion avec des lames de métal organisées comme le clavier d'un piano. Des tubes métalliques verticaux servent à faire résonner le son lorsque les lames sont percutées avec des baguettes.

This is made up of two words:

(Ger.)	*(Fr.)*	*(Eng.)*
eine Glocke	*une cloche*	a bell
spiel *(v.)* spielen	*joue (v.) jouer*	(to) play
(n.) das Spiel	*le jouet*	toy

La hallebarde – die Helmbarte *(Ger.)* halbard *(Eng.)*

A pole weapon with an axe on the end. Other variants in English: halbert or halberd

e.g.

(Ger.)	*(Fr.)*	*(Eng.)*
der Helm	*la hampe*	handle
die Barte	*la hâche*	hatchet

Une hampe à hâche (Fr.). is also used.

La hutte - die Hütte *(Ger.)* a hut *(Eng.)*

A shelter constructed using branches or straw or wattle and daub that can be used as make-shift living quarters.

Il a installé une cabane de jardin.
He installed a garden hut.

Le clayonnage en torchis (Fr.) Wattle and daub (Eng.)
l'argile (Fr.) clay *(Eng.)*

Kaputt – kaputt *(Ger.)* kaputt *(Eng.)*

(adj.) indicating that something is broken:

e.g.

Cet appareil est complétement kaputt.
This device is completely broken.

The acronym H.S. is also used in French

H.S. - Hors Service (Fr.)
pronounced *ash-es*
out of service, out of order *(Eng.)*

Le leitmotiv - das Leitmotiv *(Ger.)* leitmotif *(Eng.)*

A guiding principle. It can also be a phrase or a theme that is repeated in a musical composition or in a piece of art. In music, this repeated musical phrase can be associated with a character depicted in a story.

Peter And The Wolf, by Prokofiev [33]

*Dans l'œuvre Pierre et Le Loup, de Prokofiev, l'oiseau est représenté par un **leitmotiv** joué par une flûte traversière.*

In the Musical composition Peter and The Wolf, by Prokofiev, the bird is represented by a leitmotiv played by a flute.

Les nouilles *(pl.)* - die Nudeln *(pl.) (Ger.)* noodle(s) *(Eng.)*

Les nouilles sont typiquement faites à partir de farine de blé, de riz ou de haricots mungo.

Noodles are typically made from wheat, rice, or mung bean flour.

Un putsch - der Putsch *(Ger.)* putsch *(Eng.)*

An attempted revolution. A form of rioting with street clashes and social strife seen in post-WW1 Germany. Someone who carries out a putsch is a putschist *(Eng.)* - *un(e) putschiste (Fr.)*.

KAPP-PUTSCH[34]

KAPP-PUTSCH était une tentative échouée de coup d'état pour renverser le gouvernement de Weimar en 1920.

KAPP-PUTSCH was a failed, attempted coup to overthrow the Weimar government in 1920.

KAPP-PUTSCH is <u>not</u> related to the adjective kaputt *(Ger.)*.

Les quenelles - die Knödeln *(Ger.)* dumplings *(Eng.)*

La quenelle is a delicacy in Lyon and Alsace.

Ingrédients :
farine, eau (lait), viande (volaille ou poisson).
Ingredients:
flour, water (milk), meat (poultry or fish).

Knödeln is also linked to

(Ger.)	*(Fr.)*	*(Eng.)*	*(Lat.)*
der Knoten	*nœud*	knot	nodum

> **Schlass(e), chlass(e)** *(adj.)* – erschöpft *(Ger.)* very tired *(Eng.)*

Comes from the Alsatian language:

(adj.)	<u>a state of tiredness</u>
(Fr.)	*Elle était schlasse.*
(Eng.)	She was shattered (tired).

(adj.)	<u>or a state of drunkenness</u>
(Fr.)	*Il est chlass.*
(Eng.)	He's sloshed, drunk.

And also the noun can have two spellings:

(Fr.)	*(n.) un chlass, un schlass*
(Eng.)	a flick-knife, a penknife

Le zeitgeist - der Zeitgeist *(Ger.)* Zeitgeist *(Eng.)*

Zeitgeist[35] embodies a set of ideas, beliefs, feelings, and characteristics of society at a given period in history. It is made up of two words:

(Ger.)	*(Fr.)*	*(Eng.)*
die Zeit	*le temps*	time
der Geist	*l'esprit/ le*	spirit /
	fantôme	ghost

Zeitgeist would literally be *L'esprit du temps (Fr.)*, but the expression *L'air du temps (Fr.)* is often heard.

(Fr.)	*C'est dans l'air du temps.*
(Eng.)	It is in keeping with the times.

CHAPTER 5

English Origins

The English language's influence throughout the world correlated with the expansion of the British Empire and also the rise of the USA as an economic power.

However, the French were a mighty, powerful nation and had been rivals to the English (and then the British) for centuries. It was unlikely for the French to be receptive to the English language during this long period.

L'Entente Cordiale

The Entente Cordiale[36] of 1904 no doubt assured long-lasting peace between the French and the British. However, it was only in the latter part of the 20th century that the English language became so widely studied in France and dare we say, embraced.

No doubt, the Franco-American friendship had something to do with this.

Let's say that an avalanche of English words has been adopted into the French language.

A few words ending in *-ing* have found their way into the French language, and quite a few English words are taken as-is, although many words have been adapted to the situation. *Un short (Fr.)* is a pair of shorts. *Un T-shirt (Fr.)* is simply a t-shirt.

Le babysitter – baby-sitter

(v.) *faire du baby-sitting (Fr.)* - to babysit
The French have even adapted this to both male and female:

une babysitteuse *(nf.)*   un babysitter *(nm.)*

Someone who looks after the kids is *la nounou (Fr.)* or Nanny *(Eng.)*.

Booster – *(v.)* to boost / to reinforce

Je dois travailler plus pour booster mes résultats.
I need to work harder to boost my results.

Les baskets – casual shoes or trainers

Taken from the word basketball:

e.g.

Je préfère mettre mes baskets pour marcher en ville.
I prefer wearing trainers for walking around town.

Le driver – the driver

As in harnessed trotting racing… e.g.

Le driver a bien géré son cheval dans la course au trot attelé.
The driver controlled his horse well in the harnessed trotting race.

(v.) *driver (Fr.)*   to drive *(Eng.)*

L'homme connaît bien ce cheval. Il l'a drivé plusieurs fois.
The man knows the horse well. He has driven it on several occasions.

Faire un footing - to go for a jog

This term is widely used in French.

Tous les jours, je fais un footing dans les bois.
Every day, I go for a jog in the woods.

(Fr.)	(Eng.)
le pied	foot
le football	football

(Fr.)	*la course à pied*
(Eng.)	*running*
(Fr.)	*les chaussures de course*
(Eng.)	running shoes

Faire le forcing – to put pressure on s.o.

Je vais faire le forcing auprès de Tom, pour partir vendredi.
I'll put pressure on Tom to leave on Friday.

Flirter – *(v.)* to flirt

A more French equivalent would be

(Fr.)	*(v.) draguer*
(Eng.)	to seduce, to hit on, to chat up

L'interview – interview

The standard French word is *un entretien (Fr.)*.

> *Hier, j'ai eu une interview pour un job d'été.*
> Yesterday, I had an interview for a Summer job.

Le jockey – jockey

> *Dans la course hippique, sur quinze jockeys qui y ont participé, seuls huit ont atteint la ligne d'arrivée.*
> In the horse race, out of 15 jockeys who participated, only 8 reached the finishing line.

Le meeting – meeting

> *Je serai en meeting jusqu'à quinze heures.*
> I'll be in a meeting until 3 pm. (15:00 hours)

Mettre quelqu'un KO – to knock s.o. out

That's *KO* as in *Knock-Out*.
Je suis KO is French slang for
'I'm shattered' as in tired.

Le parking – car park

> *Elle a garé sa bagnole dans le parking.*
> She parked her car in the car park.

NB: *une bagnole* is slang for car - *une voiture (Fr.).*

Le pullover, le pull – pullover or jumper

> *Il porte son pull en laine.*
> He's wearing his wool pullover.

Punchy – forceful, striking, having punch

> *Cette femme est vraiment punchy.*
> *(percutante, dynamique)*
> That woman has spirit.

e.g.

> *Belle présentation ! Il y avait du punch.*
> Great presentation! It was very powerful.

Le rosbif – The roast-beef

Amusing that the French refer to the English as *Les Rosbifs* (The Roast Beefs).

(Fr.)	(Eng.)
(nm.) le bœuf	beef
(v.) rôtir	to roast
rôti(e)	roast**ed**
de la viande rôtie	roasted meat
un bœuf	a castrated bull
(adj.) bovin(e)	bovine
de la viande d'origine bovine	meat from bovine animals
(v.) faire le bœuf	to jam (as in music)

Le smoking – smoking jacket

L'homme porte son smoking.
The man is wearing his smoking jacket.

(Fr.)	(Eng.)
un nœud papillon	a bow tie
le papillon (n.)	the butterfly
une ceinture de smoking	a cumberbund
fumer (v.)	to smoke
un foulard de poche	a pocket square

Être snob – to be a snob

A very popular expression in French:

e.g.

Elle est trop snob cette fille.
That girl is such a snob.

Snober quelqu'un – to snub someone

Il est passé devant moi et m'a complétement snobé.
He walked past me and completely ignored me. (as in *snubbed me*)

Faire un taping – to apply kinesio tape

A term used by physiotherapists to apply kinesio tape to stabilise a part of the body.

Le kiné a fait un taping de l'épaule du patient.
The physiotherapist taped the patient's shoulder.

(Fr.)	*(n.) un(e) kinésithérapeute*
(Eng.)	a physiotherapist

Often shortened to *un(e) kiné.*

Un uppercut – an uppercut *(Eng.)*

A boxing term for a strike to the face with the fist, with an upward movement. The French distinguish between

- *la boxe anglaise* - English boxing
- *la boxe française* - a French version of kick-boxing

(Fr.)	*(Eng.)*
les gants de boxe	boxing gloves
Un coup sec	a jab

W.C. – WC or Water Closet

Pronounced '*Vay-Say*' in French.

You'll even hear '*wattair clozette'* spoken in French.

Elle est partie aux waters.
(pronounced *wattair*)
She's gone to the toilet.

les toilettes (Fr.)   the toilet *(Eng.)*

CHAPTER 6

Arabic Origins

Literally Hundreds of Arabic Words

The influence of the Arabic language on Southern European languages is significant. In French, hundreds of Arabic words are used.

There is a certain logic in this for several reasons:

- **Trade** between Mediterranean states has resulted in the borrowing of words from other languages throughout history.
- **The Umayyad invasions** took the Arab armies as far North as Poitiers, only to be defeated by Charles Martel [37] in 732 AD. Meanwhile, the influence of Arabic on South-Western European languages was well on its way.
- **French colonisation** [38] of North Africa (Algeria 1830, Tunisia 1881, French Protectorate of Morocco 1912) was no doubt made possible by the decline of the Ottoman Empire in North Africa.
- **Immigration** [39] from the Maghreb after WWII saw an influx of workers participating in France's re-industrialisation.

The phonetic [40] form is provided in the following examples:

> **L'alcazar** – al-qasr *(Ara.)* fortified palace *(Eng.)*

> *L'alcazar de Séville est un de ses monuments les plus célèbres.*
>
> The Alcazar in Seville is one of its most famous monuments.

> **L'alcool** – al-kuhul *(Ara.)* alcohol *(Eng.)*

> *En France, il est interdit pour un mineur d'acheter de l'alcool.*
>
> In France, it is forbidden for an under-age person to buy alcohol.

> **L'algèbre** – al-jabr *(Ara.)* algebra *(Eng.)*

The foundations of Algebra[41]

> The foundations of Algebra were written in a book in the early 800s (Yes! Around 1200 years ago) by a Persian mathematician **Al-khawarizmi**.
>
> Like it or not, Algebra is part of every child's education in High School.

L'algorithme – algorithm *(Eng.)*

Named after the same Persian mathematician **Al-khawarizmi** (aka algorithm). How cool is that to have your name mentioned on a day-to-day basis by millions of people throughout the world (Science, Teaching & IT and the online world).

L'azur – lazaward *(Ara.)* azure *(Eng.)*

Azur ou bleu clair décrit la couleur du ciel.
Azure or light blue describes the colour of the sky.

Bésef, bezzef *(adj.)* bezzaf *(Ara.)* lots of *(Eng.)*

A French slang term used in the negative to indicate:
C'est pas bésef!
It's not much! / It's not a lot.

Le café – qahwah *(Ara.)* coffee *(Eng.)*

The French also use the word '*caoua*' directly from Arabic.

Ça te dit de prendre un caoua ?
Do you fancy a coffee?

Une carafe – garafa *(Ara.)* a water jug *(Eng.)*

A few alternatives for *une carafe* are used in France:
Quelques alternatives pour une carafe sont utilisées en France :
Un broc, une cruche, un pot

Le coton – qutun *(Ara.)* cotton *(Eng.)*

(Fr.)	*une chemise en coton*
(Eng.)	a cotton shirt

(Fr.)	un coton tige
(Eng.)	a cotton bud

L'estragon – tarhun *(Ara.)* tarragon *(Eng.)*

L'estragon est un ingrédient important pour la sauce béarnaise.
Tarragon is an important ingredient in Bearnaise sauce.

Le Béarn est une ancienne principauté située dans le département des Pyrénées-Atlantique (64). Pau est le chef-lieu.

> The Béarn is a former principality situated in the
> *département* Pyrenées-Atlantique (64). Pau is the
> county seat.

64 refers to the postal code prefix.

(Fr.)	*le département*
(Eng.)	county

Fissa – fi sâ a *(Ara.)* straight away *(Eng.)*

This has become French slang for fast, straight away:

(Fr.)	*Je vais y aller fissa.*
(Eng.)	I'll go straight away.

La jarre – jarra *(Ara.)* jar *(Eng.)*

The French also use *le bocal (Fr.)* – jar *(Eng.)*.
The Arabic word generally refers to an earthenware jar.

Le loofah – luf *(Ara.)* loofah *(Eng.)*

---

une éponge (Fr.) a sponge *(Eng.)*

Le safran – za faran *(Ara.)* saffron *(Eng.)*

> *Contient des antioxydants et des traces
> importantes de magnésium.*

> Contains antioxidants and a high level of
> magnesium.

Le sirop – sarab *(Ara.)* syrup *(Eng.)*

Un sirop peut être un médicament à boire :

(Fr.)	*(Eng.)*
un sirop	a cough syrup, cough medicine
un sirop à l'eau	a fruit cordial

Le sucre – sukkar *(Ara.)* sugar *(Eng.)*

Interesting to note that sugar in German is *Zucker*.

Le toubib – tabib *(Ara.)* doctor *(Eng.)*

Le toubib is French slang. The standard word in French is *le docteur (Fr.)*.

Le zéro – sifr *(Ara.)* zero, nought or cipher *(Eng.)*

Zero [42] was possibly one of the most revolutionary mathematical concepts ever devised. **Brahmagupta**, an Indian mathematician came up with the concept of ZERO c.600 A.D..

Arabic mathematicians adopted the Hindu Numeral System not long after the death of the Prophet Mohammad.

It wasn't until near the end of the 900s A.D. that the *Hindu-Arabic Numeral System* started to appear in Europe.

(n.) le chiffre *(Fr.)*   raqm *(Ara.)*   number *(Eng.)*

       (Fr) *(Eng.)*
(v.) chiffrer   to calculate or to put a cost on something
  chiffré(e)   encoded or numbered

CHAPTER 7

Greek Origins

Over almost 15 centuries, Greek influence spread throughout Eastern Europe, in what is today's Middle East and North Africa. That was ample time for Greek culture to leave a significant imprint on the Mediterranean Region and Mesopotamia.

Let us consider four main periods of the numerous periods of Greek history:

- **The Mycenaean Period/Dark Ages (1600-800 B.C.)** witnessed the Trojan Wars [43]. Sparta is founded c.900 B.C.
- **Archaic Age of Greece (800-500 B.C.)** - Greek colonisation of the Mediterranean and the Black Sea. Homer writes The Iliad and Odyssey. This is the Period of the First Olympics[44] and the Persian Wars, and **Pythagoras[45].**
- **Classical Period (500-323 B.C.)** – which saw the construction of architectural wonders such as the Parthenon [46] and the works of the historian **Thucydides**. See also the **Battle of Salamis** and **Thermopylae** [47] in 480 B.C. and the film *The 300 Spartans* [48]. **Alexander The Great**, born 356 B.C., reigned between 336-323 B.C.

- **Hellenistic Greece (323-146 B.C.)** This Period starts with **Alexander The Great's** death and includes the scientific works of **Euclid** and **Archimedes**[49].

Words with Greek origins are to be found in so many languages today. Many of these languages use a prefix or a suffix taken from Greek. Here are some examples. In certain cases, the Greek Cyrillic version is provided.

> **L'abysse** *(Fr.)* άβυσσος (abyssos) abyss *(Eng.)*

abyssus *(Lat.)*

Abyss (bottomless pit) can be broken down into two parts:

a meaning without

byss from the Greek byssos meaning bottom

sans fond *(Fr.)* bottomless, unfathomed *(Eng.)*

L'académie *(Fr.)* Ακαδημία (akadêmia)　academy *(Eng.)*

academīa *(Lat.)*

L'Académie Française est chargée de normaliser la langue française.
The Académie Française is responsible for standardising the French language.

La doxa *(Fr.)* – δοκέω (dokéo)　doxa *(Eng.)*

This refers to a group of opinions that are common to a group of people and are related to a certain social behaviour.

	(Fr.)	*(Eng.)*
(v.)	*apparaître*	to appear
(v.)	*sembler*	to seem

Greek Prefixes

Aéro- *(Fr.)* ἀέρος (aéros) *(Gr.)*　aero- *(Eng.)*

aero means 'air'

	(Fr.)	*(Eng.)*
l'aéroport	airport
l'aéronef	aircraft
la bombe aérosol	aerosol (pressurized)
cours d'aérobic	aerobics lesson

66

Anthropo- *(Fr.)* anthropo- *(Eng.)*

relates to humans, e.g.

Anthropoïde (adj.) est un terme utilisé pour les primates qui ont une morphologie proche de celle d'un être humain.

Anthropoid *(adj.)* is a term used for primates having a similar morphology to humans.

L'étude de l'homme [50]

Definition of Anthropologie (Anthropology [51]) :

Définition de l'anthropologie selon Larousse :

L'étude de l'homme et des groupes humains. Théorie philosophique qui met l'homme au centre de ses préoccupations.

The study of the human race, its culture and society, and its physical development.

Anti- *(Fr.)* anti- *(Eng.)*

---

meaning *contre (Fr.)*   against *(Eng.)* , e.g.

(Fr.)	*(Eng.)*
antisocial(e)	antisocial
anticlimax	anticlimax

The expression 'to be an anticlimax' could also be translated as '*être décevant*' (to be disappointing).

Auto- *(Fr.)* auto- *(Eng.)*

---

meaning 'self', e.g.

(Fr.)	*(Eng.)*
une autobiographie	an autobiography
un autographe	an autograph
un autoportrait	a self-portrait

Chrono- *(Fr.)* chrono- *(Eng.)*

---

meaning 'time', e.g.

(Fr.)	*(Eng.)*
un chronomètre	a stopwatch
la chronologie	chronology

Dia- *(Fr.)* διά (dia) *(Gr.)* dia- *(Eng.)*

meaning 'across/beyond/through', e.g.

(Fr.)	*(Gr.)*	*(Eng.)*
le diamètre	διάμετρος	diameter
	diametros	
le dialecte	διάλεκτος	dialect
	diálektos	(discourse)
le diaphragme	διάφραγμα	diaphragm
	diaphragma	

Gastro- *(Fr.)* gastro- *(Eng.)*

(Fr.)	*(Eng.)*
le ventre	stomach
la gastronomie	gastronomy
j'ai une gastro	I've got a stomach bug

Hémi- *(Fr.)* hemi- *(Eng.)*

meaning 'half or partially', e.g.

(Fr.)	*(Eng.)*
un hémisphère	hemisphere, half-sphere

Hyper- *(Fr.)* υπερ (uper) hyper *(Eng.)*

Corresponds to 'excess' or 'above', e.g.
> *l'hypersensibilité (Fr.)*   hypersensitivity *(Eng.)*

Péri- *(Fr.)* περί (perí) *(Gr.)* peri- *(Eng.)*

(Fr.)	*(Eng.)*
autour	around
le périmètre	perimeter
la périphérie	periphery (field of view)

Poly- *(Fr.)* πολύς (polus) *(Gr.)* poly- *(Eng.)*

Meaning 'many/much/multi/several', e.g.
> *plusieurs (Fr.)*   several *(Eng.)*

Polyglotte (Fr.) signifie multilingue.
Polyglot *(Fr.)* means multi-lingual.
La glotte (Fr.) correspond à l'ouverture entre les cordes vocales.
The glottis *(Eng.)* is the opening between the vocal cords.

un polymère (Fr.) a polymer *(Eng.)*

(Fr.)	*la corde*
(Eng.)	string, rope, cord
(Lat.)	chorda

(adj.)
Polymorphe (Fr.) correspond à quelque chose qui peut avoir de multiples formes.
Polymorphous *(Eng.)* refers to something that can have multiple forms or shapes.

Sym- *(Fr.)* σύμ (sum) *(Gr.)*   sym- *(Eng.)*

avec (Fr.) with *(Eng.)*

(Fr.)	*(Eng.)*
la sympathie	sympathy
la symbiose	symbiosis
être en symbiose	to be in perfect harmony

Greek Suffixes

-cratie *(Fr.)* -κρατία (-kratía) -cracy *(Eng.)*

(Fr.)	*(Eng.)*
une forme de gouvernement	a form of government
une démocratie	a democracy
une théocratie	a theocracy

-graphie *(Fr.)* -graphy *(Eng.)*

Refers to the 'process of writing or recording or drawing or registering' or in Ancient Greek gráphein (γράφειν).

(Fr.)	(Eng.)
la biographie	biography
la cartographie	cartography
la cryptographie	cryptography
la géographie	geography
un séismographe	a seismograph

-morphe *(Fr.)* -morphous *(Eng.)*

Refers to

(Fr.)	(Eng.)
la forme	the shape or form of something
amorphe	amorphous - a feeling of apathy

Amorphous [52] - is also used in Chemistry and Geology to indicate a substance that does not have a fixed form or shape.

-ologie *(Fr.)* -ology *(Eng.)*

L'étude de .... *(Fr.)*   The study of...

e.g. *la biologie* [53] *(Fr.)*   biology *(Eng.)*

L'étude scientifique d'êtres vivants et les lois
de la vie.

The scientific study of the natural processes
of living things.

-phage *(Fr.)* -phagus *(Eng.)* - phagein *(Gr.)*

(v.) manger (Fr.)   to eat *(Eng.)*

(adj.) **chronophage** *(Fr.)*
indique que quelque chose prend beaucoup de
temps.

indicates that something is **time-consuming**.
(Eng.)

(n.) l'œsophage (Fr.) the esophagus *(Eng.)*

CHAPTER 8

Latin Origins

The Roman Influence

The Roman Empire spread from Rome to Northern Europe, Britain, Iberia, the Balkans, North Africa, the Middle East, Mesopotamia, and as far as Armenia.

It is no wonder that Latin[54] significantly influenced so many languages: from Romance languages[55] Italian, Romanian, French, Spanish, Catalan, Portuguese, and Romansch (one of the officially-recognized languages of Switzerland) to English and German.

Some of the words of Latin origin below are likely to be familiar to people who speak any of the above languages.

Take the Latin word *femina* meaning woman *(Eng.)* or *femme (Fr.)*.

The following words can often be heard in French conversation. For the most, the French use the Latin word as-is. Occasionally, it might be a derivative of the original word.

A contrario

Au contraire (Fr.) – conversely, to the contrary, instead *(Eng.)*

(Fr.)	*au contraire*
(Eng.)	conversely, to the contrary, instead

Manger trop de sucre peut avoir une incidence sur votre poids. A contrario, manger plus sainement, peut faciliter la perte de poids.
Eating too much sugar can impact your weight. Conversely, eating healthily can help with weight loss.

Ad nauseam

Used as-is in both French and English.
Refers to something done to an excessive, almost annoying degree.

Il a répété la même chose ad nauseam.

He endlessly repeated the same thing.

L'agenda *(Fr.)* – agenda *(Eng.)*

A short list of things to be done/to be dealt with.

> *(v.)* agir *(Fr.)* to act *(Eng.)* agere *(Lat.)*

Mon agenda est bien rempli pour la semaine.

My diary is full for the whole week.

Alea iacta est / alea jacta est

(Fr.)	*(Eng.)*
Le sort en est jeté	The die is cast
Les dés sont jetés	The dice have been rolled/cast
un dé	one die *(sing.)*
deux dés	two dice *(pl.)*

Un point de non-retour (Fr.) signifies that events have come to a point of no return.

The term *alea iacta est* is attributed to Ceasar in 49 BC, when, against the will of the Roman senate, he dared to cross the Rubicon [56] river with his army, thus causing a long civil war.

Amen

Amen (Lat.)   Amen *(Eng.)*

Amen comes from the Hebrew word for truth – *la verité (Fr.)*

C'est ainsi (Fr.)   It is so *(Eng.)*

Ad libitum – *(abbr.)* **Ad Lib**

        (Fr.)   *(Eng.)*

À volonté, à satiété   at one's pleasure, until satisfied

(v.) *improviser librement à sa manière*

To improvise at will

En musique c'est une invitation à l'interprète de jouer/chanter à sa manière.
In musical terms, this is an invitation to the performer to play along as they like.

It also corresponds to 'Speak freely without notes'.

A priori

Affirmation : A priori, on y arrive ce soir.
Affirmation: It's likely we'll arrive tonight.

Préjudice : Il faut éviter des à prioris.
Prejudice: We must avoid preconceptions.

Bis, ter, quater, quinquies...

Several meanings for **bis**

(Fr.)	(Eng.)
deuxième	second
deux fois	twice
deuxième fois	second time

can be used in a French address: e.g. *47**bis** rue de Caen*
indicating that the parcel of land for the original n°47 was split into
2 parcels: n°47 & n°47bis.

or similarly 18**ter** avenue Eiffel

split into 3 parcels: n°18, n°18bis & n° 18ter.

ter *(Lat.)* *trois, troisième (Fr.)*   three, third *(Eng.)*

In law, these Latin words indicate sub-paragraphs:

(Lat.)	(Fr.)	(Eng.)
bis	*second*	second
ter	*troisième*	third
quater	*quatrième*	fourth
quinquies	*cinquième*	fifth
et cetera...	*...et ainsi de suite*	...and so on

Carpe diem

profite du jour présent (Fr.) seize the day *(Eng.)*

Taken from the '*Odes* [57] ', a collection of Latin poems written by *Horatio* [58] who lived between 65 and 8 BC during the reign of the Roman Emperor *Augustus*. In the French-speaking world, *Horatio* is known as *Horace, pronounced 'O-rass'*. Here is an extract from the poem:

> *...carpe diem quam minimum credula postero.*
> **Horatio (Horace)**, Odes (ch.1, 11)

Cueille le jour présent ne faisant pas crédit à demain. Cueille le jour présent sans te soucier du lendemain. *(Fr.)*
Seize the day without worrying about the morrow *(Eng.)*.

(Fr.)	*le lendemain*
(Eng.)	the day after, the following day

Se soucier de quelque chose/quelqu'un.
To worry about something/someone.

Other translations of Carpe Diem could be:

Une incitation à la recherche du plaisir.
An encouragement towards the seeking of pleasure.

A quick time-out from the world of Latin:
What an ideal moment to segue into a focus on a
Greek philosopher....in our Latin section!

Epikouros Ἐπίκουρος (342-270 B.C.)
Epicure *(Fr.)* Epicurus *(Eng.)*

Born in the era of Alexander the Great, he was the
father of Epicureanism.

Né à l'époque d'Alexandre le Grand, il est le père de
l'Epicurisme.

Epicureanism [59] *(Eng.)* L'Epicurisme *(Fr.)*

Epicurisme est une philosophie de la recherche du plaisir par la tranquillité et le confort et l'absence de la douleur.
Epicureanism is a philosophy of seeking pleasure in the form of tranquillity and comfort and the absence of bodily pain.

Cassus belli – *cas de guerre (Fr.)* cause for war *(Eng.)*

L'assassinat du Grand-Duc Ferdinand est devenu un cassus belli pour l'Empire Austro-Hongrois en 1914.

The assassination of Grand Duke Ferdinand became a cassus belli for the Austro-Hungarian Empire in 1914.

Circa – *environ (Fr.)* approximately *(Eng.)*

à peu près, approximativement (Fr.) - approximately

circa[60] 1820 – around the year 1820

(abbr.) c.1820

Circum – *autour (Fr.)* around *(Eng.)*

(v.) circumnaviguer *(Fr.)* to circumnavigate *(Eng.)*

Magellan a été le premier à naviguer autour du globe.

Magellan was the first to circumnavigate the globe.

Credo – *(n.) le crédo (Fr.)*   creed, credo *(Eng.)*

(Fr.) *(v.)* **croire** :   Je crois
(Eng.) *(v.)* **to believe**, **to trust**:   I believe
(Lat.) *(v.)* **credere**:   credo

(Fr.) *(n.)* credence, belief
(Eng.) *(n.) la crédence, la croyance*
(Lat.) *(n.)* credentia

(Fr.) *(n.) le crédit*
(Eng.) *(n.)* credit
(Lat.) *(n.)* creditum

| *Une déclaration publique de croyances ou d'opinions (souvent religieux).* |
| A public declaration of beliefs or opinions (often religious). |

Distinguo

| *Il faudra faire le distinguo entre les deux solutions.* |
| It will be necessary to make the distinction between the two solutions. |

Ergo – *donc (Fr.)* therefore *(Eng.)*

Nous n'avons aucune option alternative. Ergo,
on sait ce qu'il nous reste à faire.

We have no other alternative. Therefore, we
know what remains to be done.

Erratum

une erreur à corriger (Fr.) - an error to be corrected *(Eng.)*

ERRATUM : cette version annule et remplace
la précédente.

ERRATUM: this version supersedes the
previous version.

Et cetera *(abbr.)* etc.

(Fr.)	*et ainsi de suite*
(Eng.)	and so on
(Ger.)	und so weiter (u.s.w.)

Il est l'heure de mettre la table : apporte les
couverts, les verres, un dessous de plat, le sel, le
poivre, etc.

It's time to set the table: bring the knives and forks,
the glasses, a trivet, the salt and pepper, etc.

Ex æquo – *à égalité (Fr.)* a draw *(Eng.)*

> *Malheureusement, c'était un vote ex æquo. La législation n'a pas pu être adoptée.*
> Unfortunately, it was a tie vote in parliament. The legislation was not passed.

> *Les deux joueurs ont fini ex æquo pour la troisième place.*
> The two players tied for third place.

Exempli gratia - e.g.[61]

This is used by the anglophone world. The French tend to use:

(Fr.)	*(Eng.)*
par exemple	for example
(abbr.) *p. ex.*	e.g.

Facsimile - *une copie exacte (Fr.)* an exact copy *(Eng.)*

The name for Fax-technology is derived from this word.
envoyer un fax (Fr.)   to send a fax *(Eng.)*

Gratis – *gratis, gratuit (Fr.)* free of charge/free *(Eng.)*

The French also use the slang version *gratos* in conversation, e.g.

Ce soir, l'entrée au cinéma est gratos.

Tonight, it's free to get in at the cinema.

Grosso modo – *grosso modo, à peu près (Fr.)*
approximately *(Eng.)*

Grosso modo, la voiture vaut dix mille euros.

The car is approximately worth ten thousand euros.

Hic *(Lat.)* – *ici (Fr.)*   here *(Eng.)*

Le hic is also used to draw attention to 'The crux of the matter'. *(Eng.)*.

le nœud de l'affaire /
l'aspect difficile /
la partie la plus difficile. (Fr.).

Hic est quaestio. *(Lat.)*.

Voilà le hic / Là est la question. (Fr.).

Here lies the crux of the matter / Here lies the question. *(Eng.)*

Il y a un hic. (Fr.)

There has been a hiccup / There is a fly in the ointment, a glitch, a hiccup, a snag. *(Eng.)*

Idem – idem *(Lat.)*

(Fr.)   *(Eng.)*
la même chose   the same thing
e.g.

Mettez le colis dans la petite pièce. Idem pour l'autre boîte.
Put the package in the small room. The same goes for the other box.

The equivalent to the use of 'ditto' in English, meaning 'as before' or '*aforesaid*'.

Incognito – *incognito (Fr.)*   incognito *(Eng.)*

(Fr.)   *sans révéler son identité*
(Eng.)   without revealing one's true identity

Je préfère utiliser mon browser en mode incognito.
I prefer using my browser in incognito mode.

In extremis *(adv.)* *de justesse (Fr.)* narrowly/barely *(Eng.)*

L'équipe locale a sauvé la mise, in extremis (à la dernière minute).
The local team saved the day on the last minute. (in extremis/on the death).

Ils ont gagné le vote in extremis.

(de justesse).

They won by a narrow majority.

Ils ont évité un accident in extremis.

They had a near miss.

In fine

(Fr.)   *En fin de compte / finalement*

(Eng.)   ultimately, in the end, when all is said and done

e.g.

Le client décidera, in fine, en fonction de son budget.

The customer will ultimately choose according to their budget.

Ipso facto – *par le fait même* *(Fr.)* by the very fact *(Eng.)*

*Si le gouvernement perd cette circonscription, il perd sa majorité, **ipso facto**.*

If the government loses that constituency, ipso facto (automatically), they lose their majority.

La libido – le désir (sexuel) *(Fr.)* desire *(Eng.)*

Il existe des remèdes naturels pour augmenter la libido (le désir sexuel).

There are natural remedies to increase the libido (sexual desire).

Mea culpa – mon erreur, ma faute *(Fr.)* my error, my fault, my mistake *(Eng.)*

(Fr.)   *L'aveu de la faute commise*
(Eng.)   The admission of guilt

e.g.

Hier, j'ai fait mon mea culpa devant mon ami.

Yesterday, I apologised to my friend.

> **Nec plus ultra** – *ce qu'il y a de mieux (Fr.)* the very best of the best *(Eng.)*

(Lat.)	*(Fr.)*	*(Eng.)*
nec	*ne…ni…*	neither…nor…
plus	*plus*	more
ultra	*un degré extrême*	an extreme degree

e.g.

> *J'ai essayé plein de produits de nettoyage.*
> *Celui-ci est vraiment **le nec plus ultra**.*

> I've tried lots of cleaning products. This one is the very best of the best.

> **Nota** – Nota *(Fr.)* Nota Bene [62] *(Eng.)*

The initials N.B. are used in English, indicating a note made in the margin of a text or simply an additional item of information at the end of a letter. e.g.

C'est utilisé dans plusieurs contextes :
- ajouter un point supplémentaire à la fin d'une lettre ou d'une observation ou remarque dans un document.

It is used in several contexts:
- to add an additional item of information at the end of a letter or an observation or remark in a document.

> **Le parabellum** – die Parabellum *(Ger.)* parabellum *(Eng.)*

Parabellum [63] comes from the Latin:

(Lat.)	(Fr.)	(Ger.)	(Eng.)	(It.)
para	*préparer*	vorbereiten	prepare	*preparare*
bellum	*la guerre*	der Krieg	war	*la guerra*
bellicus	*belliqueux*	krieglustig	belligerent	*bellicoso*
	belliqueuse			

"si vis pacem, para bellum"

Publius Flavius Vegetius Renate [64]

If you want peace, prepare for war.

Si tu veux la paix, prépare-toi pour la guerre.

The original Parabellum [65]

> The original Parabellum was a self-loading handgun designed by Hugo Borchardt in 1893.
>
> One of his engineers, Georg **Lugar**, made an improved version that became known as *Die Pistole 08* or the *Parabellum P08*.
>
> It was used in the German Navy from 1903 and then the German Army from 1908. It is one of the most iconic handguns.

Post scriptum *(abbr.)* **PS**

(Fr.)   *(Eng.)*

écrit après   written after

ce qui est ajouté à une lettre après la signature.

that which is added at the end of a letter after the signature.

Le quiproquo *(Fr.)* Quid pro quo *(Lat.)* / *(Eng.)*

(Fr.)   *une chose contre une autre*

(Eng.)   an exchange of one thing against another

(Fr.)   *un accord réciproque*

(Eng.)   a reciprocal agreement

In French, it is often used to indicate

(Fr.)   *une erreur*

(Eng.)   an error

(Fr.)   un malentendu

(Eng.)   a misunderstanding

e.g.

Confondre une personne avec une autre.

To mistake one person for another.

Refer to the *Quid pro quo*[66] in the play **L'avare** by Molière.

(Fr.)	(Eng.)
(n) l'avare	miser
(v) être avare	to be miserly

Recto

Indicates the side of a sheet of paper that is to be read first.

Indique le côté d'une feuille qui doit être lu en premier.

Verso

signifie l'autre côté de la feuille.

represents the other side of the sheet of paper.

Recto-verso signifie les deux côtés d'une feuille.

Recto-verso signifies both sides of a sheet of paper.

Numismatic context

The front side of a coin is the Obverse.

The other side of a coin is the Reverse.

(Fr.)   *(Eng.)*
l'avers (pile)   obverse (heads)
le revers (face)   reverse (tails)
pile ou face   heads or tails

Le Requiem – requiem *(Eng.)*

Une prière pour les morts ou une messe de funérailles.
A prayer for the dead or a funeral mass.

Requiscat in pace *(abbr.)* **R.I.P.**

(Fr.)   *(Eng.)*
repose en paix   Rest In peace

Requiscat *(sing.)*
(Fr.)   *Qu'il/elle repose en paix*
(Eng.)   May he/she rest in peace

Requiscant *(pl.)*
(Fr.)   *Qu'ils/elles reposent en paix*
(Eng.)   May they rest in peace

On a tombstone in a French cemetery, you may occasionally see the words
Ci-gît… *(Fr.)* pronounced "*see jee*" Here lies… *(Eng.)* *hic jacet… (Lat.)*

Sine die

(Fr.)	sans fixer le jour
(Eng.)	without specifying the day

e.g.

Le meeting a été repoussé **sine die**.
The meeting has been pushed back until further notice.

Sine qua non

Used as-is in French and English

La condition sans laquelle cela ne pourrait pas être. (Fr.)
indicates that something or a condition is essential or absolutely indispensable.

(Lat.)	(Fr.)	(Eng.)
sine	sans	without
qua	laquelle	which way, as
non	ne...pas	not

Tabula rasa – *table rase (Fr.)* clean slate *(Eng.)*

On fait table rase du passé et on recommence.
Let's put the past behind us and start afresh.
Let's wipe the slate clean.

CHAPTER 9

Old Norse Origins

The Vikings made a huge impact on most Northern European countries.

They invaded and eventually settled in most of Eastern Britain and made several assaults on Northern France and Paris in 845 and 885 AD. Normandy came under the influence of the Viking warlord Rollo [67].

The Vikings [68] gradually became Normans [69]. The name Normandy reflects the North Men settlers.

Several generations later, William was born. William The Conqueror went to England to claim his crown in 1066 and the rest is history.

Le Vieux Norrois

The French refer to the Old Norse language as **Vieux Norrois**. Here are a few examples of Old Norse words that crept into the French language:

Le bec – bekkur *(ONor.)*   brook *(Eng.)*   der Bach *(Ger.)*

Another similar French word is *le ruisseau (Fr.)* stream *(Eng.)*.

On a utilisé un tronc d'arbre pour traverser le bec.
We used a log to cross over the stream.

Brun – brunn *(ONor.)* brown *(Eng.)* braun *(Ger.)*

The French also use *marron (Fr.)* - brown *(Eng.)*

Le crabe – krabi *(ONor.)* crab *(Eng.)* der Krebs *(Ger.)*

(Fr.)	*(Eng.)*
le crabe araignée	spider crab
une langouste	crayfish or tiny lobster

L'étrave – stafn *(ONor.)*   stem of a boat *(Eng.)* der Steven *(Ger.)*

L'étrave[70]

L'étrave est l'extrémité avant de la coque.
The stem or bow is situated in the most forward part of a ship.

Le homard – hummar *(ONor.)* lobster *(Eng.)* der Hummer *(Ger.)*

> Le homard a deux grandes pinces.
> The lobster has two big claws.

La mare – marr *(ONor.)* pond *(Eng)*

(Fr.)	une étendue d'eau stagnante
(Eng.)	body of stagnant water
(Ger.)	der Tümpel

> La mare attire des canards et des cygnes.
> The pond attracts ducks and swans.

Le nord – nordr *(ONor.)* North *(Eng.)* der Norden *(Ger.)*

L'est – austr *(ONor.)* East *(Eng.)* der Osten *(Ger.)*

Le sud – sudr *(ONor.)* South *(Eng.)* der Süden *(Ger.)*

L'ouest – vestr *(ONor.)* West *(Eng.)* der Westen *(Ger.)*

Un renne – *hrein (ONor.)* reindeer *(Eng.)* das Ren *(Ger.)*

> Les rennes vivent dans l'hémisphère nord au Canada, en Laponie et en Sibérie.
> Reindeer are found in the Northern Hemisphere in Canada, Lapland, and Siberia.

CHAPTER 10

Japanese Origins

The Japanese culture has a distinct and strong identity, no doubt helped by centuries of relative isolation from the rest of the world.

> *Le Japon est le pays du soleil levant.*
> Japan is the Land of the Rising Sun.

Japan is well-known for its art, calligraphy, music, food, religious temples, its highly conservative and technologically-advanced society, its reputation as a once powerful military empire, its current economic might, and of course, its language.

In more recent times, it has made its mark in the Cinema and also graphic novels, known as **Mangas**.

Geographically speaking, Japan is an archipelago[71], made up of 6.852 islands. It is situated on the Pacific Ocean and lies on the infamous 'Ring Of Fire', where earthquakes and volcanic eruptions are common. On March 11 2011, a huge earthquake took place off the coast of Fukushima[72]. Then followed an enormous tsunami that caused serious damage to the Fukushima nuclear reactor.

Here are some examples of Japanese words you will often hear in French:

Un emoji – an emoji *(Eng.)*

A form of shorthand often used as a reaction in modern social media messaging. The French also use the acronym s.m.s. (short message service) text messaging, e.g.

Un dessin ou icône ou image pour exprimer un sentiment dans un message texte sur les réseaux sociaux.
A unique drawing/icon/image used in text messaging to express a sentiment or a feeling.

(Fr.)	(Eng.)
la sténographie	shorthand
des réseaux sociaux	social media
un sms	a text message
la messagerie instantanée	instant messaging

Un futon – *un lit japonais (Fr.)* Japanese bed *(Eng.)*

A futon consists of a wooden base - *le sommier (Fr.)* - and a mattress - *un matelas (Fr.)* - stuffed with layers of cotton - *le coton (Fr.)* . The bed base - *le sommier (Fr.)* - can sometimes be adjusted and the mattress folded to become a sofa - *un canapé / un sofa (Fr.)*.

Un judoka - a judoka[73] *(Eng)*

Quelqu'un qui pratique l'art martial du judo.
Someone who practises the martial art of Judo.

Un katana – a katana *(Eng.)*

Un sabre japonais utilisé par un samouraï.
A Japanese sword used by a samurai.

Un manga - a manga [74] *(Eng.)*

A term already used in 18th century Japan. This referred to a print.

This term was adopted for the more modern-day graphic novels from the 20th century onward. Manga graphic novels and films have a huge following throughout the world. In much of the French-speaking world, the Manga is a highly respected art form.

(Fr.)	*(Eng.)*
le XVIIIe siècle	the 18th century
une estampe	a print
une bande dessinée	a graphic novel

Le Nippon - Nippon [75] *(Eng.)*

Nippon is the name the Japanese give to their country

(Fr.)	*(Eng.)*
(adj.) nippon,	nippon
nipponne	

Un adjectif pour décrire quelque chose qui est japonais.
An adjective to describe something that is Japanese.

L'origami - *origami* [76] *(Eng.)*

This is the traditional Japanese art of folding paper into different artistic shapes, often animals.

These shapes can either be two- or three-dimensional.

(Jap.)	*(Fr.)*	*(Eng.)*
Oru	*le pliage*	folding
Kami	*le papier*	paper

(Fr.)	*(Eng.)*
(n.) un pli	a fold
(v.) plier	to fold
(n.) une forme	a shape

(v.) se croiser les bras
to fold one's arms

Figuratively

(n.) céder (Fr.)   to fold, to give in *(Eng.)*

Un samouraï – a samurai *(Eng.)*

Un guerrier japonais au service d'un seigneur.
A Japanese warrior who is in the service of a Lord or Master.

	(Fr.)	*(Eng.)*
(n.)	*un guerrier*	a warrior
(f.)	*une guerrière*	a female warrior

Un tsunami – a tsunami *(Eng.)*

A tsunami [77]

Un tsunami est une série de vagues provoquée par un tremblement de terre ou une éruption volcanique souterraine.

A tsunami is a series of waves caused by an earthquake or an underground volcanic eruption.

CHAPTER 11

Hindi Origins

France was present on the Indian subcontinent as early as 1668 in Surat. Surat is part of the modern-day coastal state of Gujarat, which lies on the Arabian Sea and borders   Pakistan.
In the 1660s, the Indian Moghul granted *La Compagnie Française des Indes Orientales* the rights to set up the *Comptoir de Surat*. The company name would translate to The French East-Indies Company.

However, in the late 1600s and 1700s, five main *comptoirs* [78] or Trading Posts were set up in

- Pondicherry in 1674 in Tamil Nadu
- Chandernagore 1686, known as Chandanaggar in West Bengal
- Mahé (1721) in Kerala
- Yanaon (1725), today known as Yanam in the state of Andhra Pradesh in the Bay of Bengal
- Karikal (1739), now part of Tamil Nadu

Karikal is on the Coromandel coast.

> Have you read this superb adventure
> book?
> *Coromandel!*
> by John Masters (1955)

It's interesting to know that certain of these territories were integrated into the independent nation of India several years <u>after</u> the official independence day in 1947.

The presence of The French East-Indies Company along with French Troops and exported goods to France were conducive to a cultural exchange and certain Hindi words eventually found their way into the French language.

Here are just a few:

Un avatar [79] - avatar *(Eng.)*

> *Un changement, une métamorphose, une*
> *incarnation du dieu hindou Vichnou.*
> A change, a metamorphosis, an incarnation
> of the Hindu God Vishnu.

> *Un personnage que l'on peut choisir pour se*
> *représenter dans un contexte en ligne :*
> ***p. ex.** un jeu vidéo ou un forum.*
> A character that one can choose to represent
> oneself in an online context:
> **e.g.** a computer game or a forum.

Un bungalow – bangla *(Hin.)* a bungalow *(Eng.)*

This term comes form the Gujarati word *bangalo*.
The French also use the term *plain-pied*, indicating a
construction built fully on one level at the ground level.

> *Un bungalow est un logement de plain-pied.*
> A bungalow is a dwelling built on one level.

(Fr.)	*(Eng.)*	*(Lat.)*
plain	flat, plain surface	planus

Le gourou – guru *(Eng.)*

(Fr.) *(Eng.)*
un maître spirituel *a spiritual master*
un enseignant a teacher

This is also used today to distinguish a person as a master in his/her field.

Toutes les croyances finiront par s'évanouir. La réalité seule perdurera.
All beliefs will eventually disappear. Reality alone will remain.

Sadhguru [80]

Le karma [81] - karma *(Eng.)*

This is a concept from the Hindu faith that describes the energy a person generates (positive or negative). That energy can induce or attract situations back to that person in the form of reaping rewards (positive act/positive energy) or suffering the consequences (negative act/negative energy),

e.g.

On récolte ce que l'on sème.
What goes around, comes around / You reap what you sow.

(Fr.)	(Eng.)
(v.) semer	to sow
la récolte	the harvest
l'énergie positive	positive energy
l'énergie négative	negative energy

Le punch – panch *(Hin.)* punch *(Eng.)*

Panch *(Hin.)* means five *(Eng.)* or *cinq* *(Fr.)* as in the number. It is the name given to a refreshing cocktail made up of five exotic ingredients. The French pronunciation sounds more like there is a letter 'o' instead of the 'u'.

The drink 'Punch' goes back to the 1600s and is associated with India. English (British) sailors and members of the British East India Company adopted and adapted the drink to their own tastes over the years.

Les ingrédients typiques de l'époque étaient l'alcool (cognac), du sucre roux, du jus de citron vert, de l'eau et des épices.
The typical ingredients at the time were: alcohol (brandy), brown sugar, lime juice, water, and spices.

Il existait aussi une variété de versions sans alcool.
There were also a variety of non-alcoholic versions.

Here's how to count from zero to five in Hindi:

(Hin.)	(Hin.)	(Fr.)	(Eng.)	
०	शून्य (shunya)	*zéro*	zero	0
१	एक (ek)	*un*	one	1
२	दो (do)	*deux*	two	2
३	तीन (tīn)	*trois*	three	3
४	चार (cār)	*quatre*	four	4
५	पांच (pāṅc)	*cinq*	**five**	**5**

Punch (or *Poonch* [82]) is also a town in Pakistan in the region of Kashmir on the line of control in the region disputed by Pakistan and India.

Le pyjama – pae jama *(Hin.)* pyjamas *(Eng.)*

It is a loose, light, slack pair of trousers to cover the legs. These were adopted in Western culture at the end of the 1800s. e.g.

> *Je porte un pyjama au lit.*
> I wear pyjamas for bed.

E p i l o g u e

You've just been on a journey of discovery of certain foreign words that have found their way into the French language.

As with all languages, French is a blend of many different languages and dialects and has evolved over time, influenced by a variety of historical events.

In a world where freedom of movement of people is on the increase, future outside influences are likely to continue to have an impact on the French language.

The beauty of a language is that it is a living organism and feeds on many factors, including emigration and immigration, culture, technology, and the youth.

We hope you've unearthed some interesting facts in this book and that this will spur you on and breathe new life into your linguistic adventure.

It is by no means exhaustive, but it has hopefully been an opportunity for you to step off the beaten track.
We hope you find motivation in this book to continue your journey.

Acknowledgments

Special thanks go out to those who helped make this happen: la Mif, the *Siebeneicheners*, *The Cham Crew*, *JLT-PLT*, *Thé.UK*, *The Beauties*, *The Dagonix*.

Thank you so much for your encouragement, your patience, your insight, your constructive criticism, and of course your brutal honesty, which I cherish dearly.

E-book and Audiobook Cover "TONGUE" image - courtesy of iStockphoto.com
Man's Eye "Analogicus" image - courtesy of PIXABAY
Human Ears "Shutter_Speed" image - courtesy of PIXABAY

Please Leave a Review

If you have already downloaded the **book** on Amazon, please feel free to leave us a review.

We would love to have feedback from you.

We aim to please.

If we can make improvements in any way, please let us know by sending an email to

contact@neo-urban-tongue.com

and we'll be on the case.

Our goal is to provide you with great communication tools and also an insight into various cultural aspects of the French language and French-speaking peoples.

How to Become a Subscriber

If you'd like to go on a

French Slang Learning Journey

you can subscribe to our list here:

https://frenchslang.neo-urban-tongue.com/foreignorigins?t=paper_FWFO

Resources

[1] *Why French Matters – World Languages and Cultures.* (2017, December 4). https://foreignlanguages.camden.rutgers.edu/french/why-french-matters/

[2] *Neighbouring countries of France - Neighbouring-countries.com.* (n.d.). http://www.neighbouring-countries.com/neighbouring-countries-of-france.html

[3] Pariona, A. (2017, August 16). *What Languages Are Spoken in France?* WorldAtlas. https://www.worldatlas.com/articles/what-languages-are-spoken-in-france.html

[4] Little, B. (2022, September 14). *How Far Did Ancient Rome Spread?* HISTORY. https://www.history.com/news/ancient-roman-empire-map-julius-caesar-conquests

[5] Dossena, E. (2013, September 19). *TOP TEN REASONS TO LEARN ITALIAN.* Princeton University - Italian. https://blogs.princeton.edu/italian/2013/08/29/top-ten-reasons-to-learn-italian/

[6] Tumminelli, P. (2022). *Italian Design.* SpringerLink. https://link.springer.com/chapter/10.1007/978-981-16-8782-2_15?error=cookies_not_supported&code=81a7975f-6210-44df-87b0-b570239157ce

[7] artst. (n.d.). *Italian Architects.* ARTST. https://www.artst.org/italian-architects/

[8] Larousse, Ã. (n.d.-c). *Traduction : bancarotta - Dictionnaire italien-français Larousse*. https://www.larousse.fr/dictionnaires/italien-francais/bancarotta/7748

[9] *Italian musical terms*. (n.d.). Musicca. https://www.musicca.com/musical-terms

[10] *Daube provençale*. (2000, February 20). Marmiton. https://www.marmiton.org/recettes/recette_daube-provencale_11978.aspx

[11] *What is the Venice Carnival*. (n.d.). Venice Carnival. Retrieved July 22, 2022, from https://www.venice-carnival-italy.com/what-is-the-venice-carnival/

[12] *MC Solaar Biography, Songs, & Albums*. (n.d.). AllMusic. https://www.allmusic.com/artist/mc-solaar-mn0000217328/biography

[13] *Hosea: The Book of Hosea*. (n.d.). https://www.biblehub.com/hosea/

[14] English-Language Editor: John R. Bopp. (2020, December 20). *The Incredible Revival of the Basque Language in France*. About Basque Country. https://aboutbasquecountry.eus/en/2020/05/15/the-incredible-revival-of-the-basque-language-in-france/

[15] Pons, M. (2022, February 26). *Why did Aran, with Occitan cultural roots, become part of the Catalan world?* In English. https://www.elnacional.cat/en/culture/aran-occitan-roots-catalan-world-history_717519_102.html

[16] History.com Editors. (2022, August 3). *Henry VIII*. HISTORY. https://www.history.com/topics/british-history/henry-viii

[17] Cambridge Dictionary. (2022e). *embargo definition: 1. an order to temporarily stop something, especially trading or giving information: 2. to. . .. Learn more*. https://dictionary.cambridge.org/dictionary/english/embargo

[18] Khalad, K. (2022, August 5). *FERIA DE BAYONNE: que la fête recommence !* ZEITBLATT Magazin. https://zeitblatt.com/feria-de-bayonne-que-la-fete-recommence/

[19] *The Sun Also Rises*. (n.d.). Goodreads. https://www.goodreads.com/book/show/3876.The_Sun_Also_Rises

[20] NEO URBAN TONGUE. (2022, August 3). *List Of Herbs And Spices - NEO URBAN TONGUE*. NEO URBAN TONGUE - Listen. Learn. Interact. Connect. https://neo-urban-tongue.com/list-of-herbs-and-spices/

[21] *The History and Origin Of Hammocks*. (2021, October 3). Hamacama. https://www.hamacama.com/en/history-and-origin-of-the-hammock/

[22] *The History of Corn – From Wild Grain to Staple Crop*. (2021, April 5). Many Eats – Recipes, Equipment, and Cooking Methods. https://manyeats.com/history-of-corn/

[23] Andrews, E. (2018, August 31). *Was Magellan the first person to circumnavigate the globe?* HISTORY. https://www.history.com/news/was-magellan-the-first-person-to-circumnavigate-the-globe

[24] Portuguese Trade and International Relations. Encyclopedia of Latin American History and Culture. . Retrieved December 20, 2022 from Encyclopedia.com: https://www.encyclopedia.com/humanities/encyclopedias-almanacs-transcripts-and-maps/portuguese-trade-and-international-relations

[25] Low, S. (2020, November 7). *The Portuguese in Japan*. Portuguese in Asia. https://www.portuguese.asia/post/the-portuguese-in-japan

[26] *Lusitanien*. (2022, September 15). planeteanimal.com. https://www.planeteanimal.com/chevaux/lusitanien.html

[27] Sinc, A. (2015, September 3). *The mystery of Spain's extinct zebra-like horses.* EL PAÃS English Edition. https://english.elpais.com/elpais/2015/08/27/inenglish/1440688517_4747 20.html

[28] *Napoleonic Wars - New World Encyclopedia.* (n.d.). https://www.newworldencyclopedia.org/entry/Napoleonic_Wars

[29] The Editors of Encyclopaedia Britannica. (1998b, July 20). *Franco-German War | History, Causes, & Results.* Encyclopedia Britannica. https://www.britannica.com/event/Franco-German-War

[30] Winkler, H. A. (2021, January 18). *1871: Founding of the German Reich.* deutschland.de. https://www.deutschland.de/en/topic/politics/founding-of-the-german-reich

[31] *The Alemannic Language – The Swiss Spectator.* (n.d.). https://www.swiss-spectator.ch/the-alemannic-language/

[32] *How to Play a Glockenspiel (with Pictures).* (2022, October 30). wikiHow. https://www.wikihow.com/Play-a-Glockenspiel

[33] *Pierre et le loup: travail de compréhension et de vocabulaire.* (n.d.). Derriere La Porte De Ma Classe. http://derrierelaportedemaclasse.eklablog.com/pierre-et-le-loup-travail-de-comprehension-et-de-vocabulaire-a203154092

[34] The Editors of Encyclopaedia Britannica. (2013, May 16). *Kapp Putsch | German history.* Encyclopedia Britannica. https://www.britannica.com/event/Kapp-Putsch

[35] Cambridge Dictionary. (2022a). *zeitgeist definition: 1. the general set of ideas, beliefs, feelings, etc. that is typical of a particular period in. . .. Learn more.* https://dictionary.cambridge.org/dictionary/english/zeitgeist

[36] The Editors of Encyclopaedia Britannica. (2022, April 1). *Entente Cordiale | European history.* Encyclopedia Britannica. https://www.britannica.com/event/Entente-Cordiale

[37] Hit, H. (n.d.). *Who Was Charles Martel? A Short Biography.* History Hit. https://www.historyhit.com/who-was-charles-martel/

[38] Shvili, J. (2021, December 1). *Second French Colonial Empire.* WorldAtlas. https://www.worldatlas.com/geography/second-french-colonial-empire.html

[39] *France | History, Map, Flag, Population, Cities, Capital, & Facts.* (2023, January 4). Encyclopedia Britannica. https://www.britannica.com/place/France/Immigration

[40] firdaous.com, firdaous.com, firdaous.com, firdaous.com, & firdaous.com. (n.d.-b). *Dictionnaire français arabe avec traduction phonétique* https://fr.arabia24.org/0023-dictionnaire-francais-arabe-avec-traduction-phonetique/

[41] *The History of Algebra.* (2017, April 22). ThoughtCo. https://www.thoughtco.com/the-history-of-algebra-1788145

[42] Mayer, J. (2020, March 5). *The Origin Of The Word 'Zero.'* Science Friday. https://www.sciencefriday.com/articles/the-origin-of-the-word-zero/

[43] History.com Editors. (2019, September 11). *Trojan War.* HISTORY. https://www.history.com/topics/ancient-history/trojan-war

[44] MakeDigitalYourGoal, N. (2021, August 9). *So What Are Olympic Medals Really Made Of ? | Make Digital Your Goal*. Make Digital Your Goal | Create Your Own New Digital Lifestyle. https://makedigitalyourgoal.com/so-what-are-olympic-medals-really-made-of/

[45] *Pythagorean Theorem Calculator*. (n.d.). https://www.calculator.net/pythagorean-theorem-calculator.html

[46] Cartwright, M. (2022, July 25). *Parthenon*. World History Encyclopedia. https://www.worldhistory.org/parthenon/

[47] Sommerville, D. (2022, November 2). *Battle of Thermopylae | Date, Location, and Facts*. Encyclopedia Britannica. https://www.britannica.com/event/Battle-of-Thermopylae-Greek-history-480-BC

[48] *The 300 Spartans (1962)*. (n.d.). IMDb. https://www.imdb.com/title/tt0055719/

[49] The Editors of Encyclopaedia Britannica. (1998a, July 20). *Archimedes' Principle | Description & Facts*. Encyclopedia Britannica. https://www.britannica.com/science/Archimedes-principle

[50] Larousse, Ã. (n.d.-a). *Définitions : anthropologie - Dictionnaire de français Larousse*. https://www.larousse.fr/dictionnaires/francais/anthropologie/3893

[51] Cambridge Dictionary. (2022c). *anthropology definition: 1. the study of the human race, its culture and society, and its physical development 2. the study. . .. Learn more*. https://dictionary.cambridge.org/dictionary/english/anthropology

[52] Cambridge Dictionary. (2022b). *amorphous definition: 1. (of a physical thing) having no fixed form or shape: 2. (of an idea, a plan, etc.) having no. . ..*

Learn more.

https://dictionary.cambridge.org/dictionary/english/amorphous

[53] Cambridge Dictionary. (2022d). *biology definition: 1. the scientific study of the*

natural processes of living things: 2. the scientific study of the. . .. Learn

more. https://dictionary.cambridge.org/dictionary/english/biology

[54] Janson, T. (2004). *A Natural History of Latin.* Google Books.

https://books.google.fr/books?id=4FcNoHVUwHkC

[55] Solodow, J. B. (2010). *Latin Alive: The Survival Of Latin In English And The*

Romance Languages. Google Books.

https://books.google.fr/books?id=Q6UgAwAAQBAJ

[56] *Jan 10, 49 BC: Caesar Crosses the Rubicon | National Geographic Society.*

(n.d.). https://education.nationalgeographic.org/resource/caesar-crosses-

rubicon/

[57] Eberhart, L. (2020, June 13). *Horatian Ode.* Poetry Forms.

https://poetscollective.org/poetryforms/horation-ode/

[58] Grant, M. (2022, November 27). *Horace | Roman poet.* Encyclopedia Britannica.

https://www.britannica.com/biography/Horace-Roman-poet

[59] *Hedonism and Epicureanism: most important DIFFERENCES.* (n.d.). Education,

Study and Knowledge. https://nairaquest.com/en/topics/1850-hedonism-

and-epicureanism-most-important-differences

[60] circa. (n.d.). In *The Merriam-Webster.com Dictionary.* https://www.merriam-

webster.com/dictionary/circa

[61] Cambridge Dictionary. (2023). *e.g. definition: 1. abbreviation for exempli gratia: a Latin phrase that means "for example". It can be pronounced. . .. Learn more.* https://dictionary.cambridge.org/dictionary/english/eg

[62] Larousse, Ã. (n.d.-b). *Définitions : nota, nota bene - Dictionnaire de français Larousse.* https://www.larousse.fr/dictionnaires/francais/nota/55039

[63] *Origin and meaning of parabellum.* (n.d.). Etymonline. https://www.etymonline.com/word/parabellum

[64] si vis pacem, para bellum. (n.d.-b). In *The Merriam-Webster.com Dictionary.* https://www.merriam-webster.com/dictionary/si%20vis%20pacem%2C%20para%20bellum

[65] *Luger "Parabellum" Pistol - P08.* (2018, October 14). Modern Firearms. https://modernfirearms.net/en/handguns/handguns-en/germany-semi-automatic-pistols/luger-parabellum-eng/

[66] *Quiproquo.* (n.d.). https://www.etudes-litteraires.com/figures-de-style/quiproquo.php

[67] Gange-Hrólfr 'Rollo' Ragnvaldsson. (2022, April 26). Geni_Family_Tree. https://www.geni.com/people/Gange-Hr%C3%B3lfr-Rollo-Ragnvaldsson/2915061R

[68] Man, O. T. F. (2020, May 25). *Facts About the Vikings In France, And How They Became the Normans.* 200 Facts About the Vikings. https://vikingsfacts.com/vikings-in-normandy-france-facts/

[69] Mark, J. J. (2022a, November 6). *Rollo of Normandy.* World History Encyclopedia. https://www.worldhistory.org/Rollo_of_Normandy/

[70] Ted. (2021, October 22). *Etrave - Définition - où ? - quelles formes ? - 3 exemples pratiques*. Barreatribord. https://a-la-voile.fr/etrave-definition-ou-quelles-formes-exemples-pratiques/

[71] Earth from Space: The Japanese archipelago. (n.d.). https://www.esa.int/Applications/Observing_the_Earth/Earth_from_Space_The_Japanese_archipelago

[72] Official Fukushima Travel Info - Fukushima Travel. (n.d.). https://fukushima.travel/

[73] Olympic Games(2020) https://olympics.com/en/olympic-games/tokyo-2020/results/judo

[74] Arnold, C. (2022, May 27). The History of Manga: Leading up to Modern Manga. Japan Centric. https://www.japancentric.com/the-history-of-manga-leading-up-to-modern-manga/

[75] Larousse, Ã. (n.d.-a). Définitions : nippon - Dictionnaire de français Larousse. https://www.larousse.fr/dictionnaires/francais/nippon/54625

[76] Origami - Vikidia, l'encyclopédie des 8-13 ans. (n.d.). https://fr.vikidia.org/wiki/Origami

[77] What is a tsunami? (n.d.). https://oceanservice.noaa.gov/facts/tsunami.html

[78] *11 Comptoirs des Indes | Les établissement de l' Inde | Le Petit Manchot | histoire patrimoine personnage*. (n.d.). https://www.le-petit-manchot.fr/11-comptoirs-des-indes/les-colonies-francaises/articles/941/

[79] *Définition Avatar*. (n.d.). Le Robert Dico En Ligne. Retrieved December 21, 2022, from https://dictionnaire.lerobert.com/definition/avatar

[80] B. (2021, November 14). *10 citations d'un leader : Sadhguru*. Le Blog Du Leadership. https://leblogduleadership.com/dix-citations-dun-leader-sadhguru/

[81] Olivelle, P. (2023, January 16). *Karma | Indian philosophy*. Encyclopedia

Britannica. https://www.britannica.com/topic/karma

[82] The Editors of Encyclopaedia Britannica. (1998c, July 20). *Punch | Meaning,*

Kashmir, History, & Facts. Encyclopedia Britannica.

https://www.britannica.com/place/Punch-India

Printed in Great Britain
by Amazon

39079276R00076